SOUTHSIDE RAIN

SOUTHSIDE RAIN

Quraysh Ali Lansana

THIRD WORLD PRESS, Chicago

Third World Press, P.O. Box 19730, Chicago IL 60619
Copyright © 1999 by Quraysh Ali Myles Lansana

First Edition

Cover Design: Nicole M. Mitchell
Cover Artwork: Orishegun Olomidun
Back Photo: Brooke Collins

04 03 02 01 00 99   5 4 3 2 1

ISBN 0-88378-219-7
Library of Congress Catalog Card Number 99-75732

"learning to swim" was published in *Powerlines: A Decade of Poetry
from Chicago's Guild Complex,* "passage" was published in *A Piece
of Peace: A Peace Museum Anthology* and *Pearl*; "window" was pub-
lished in *Hammers*; "71st & King Drive" was published in *Freedom
Rag Magazine*; "southside rain," "crescent, ok.," and "san antonio
blue" were published in *Atelier*; "the night before tomorrow" and
"playing hooky in alsip" were published in *Jackleg Press #1*; "afrikan
patchwork" was published in *Tomorrow Magazine*; "icons" was pub-
lished in *Eighty Gifts: In Celebration of Gwendolyn Brooks' 80th
Birthday*; "postcard from bridgeport" and "poem for queen mother"
were published in *Warpland* and "way down south" was published in
Chicago Cherry, "visiting" is an exquisite corpse co-authored by
Rachel Beck.

Livicated to

Minnie Myles King
Marie "Aunt Ree" Adams
Ernestine "Aunt Ommie" Hill
Aunt Rubie Hooper
Cousin Leroy Green
Henry Blakely II
Oscar "BoBo" Brown III
Fred Hopkins
Naikwa Jawole Nini Tasleem Nurullah
Isaiah Drew Turcotte
Tok Nakamoto

contents

section three: fortune in their eyes

section four: on things unborn

acknowledgements

Thanks and Praises due to The Creator of All Things for guidance and abundant blessings, which manifest in the following ways: my soulflower, Emily Hooper Lansana, for unending love and support; Nile Elazar Myles Lansana, Son of Olukun, Bearer of the Spear & Onan Jahleel Myles Lansana, the One with Strong Hope in God; the Myles/Lawrence Clan and the Hooper/Jenkins Posse; His Royal Highness Chief Khalilu of Moselolo, Gwendolyn Brooks, Haki Madhubuti, Reverend Dr. Jeremiah A. Wright Jr., Michael Warr, Shanta, Sista Zahra, DJ Brooks, J. Love, Tyehimba Jess and Mark Turcotte for direction; Orisegun Olomidun for friendship & art, and Niki Mitchell for wide creative eyes. For support and inspiration, I must thank, Kalumu ya Salaam, Luis Rodriguez, Reginald Gibbons, Afaa Michael Weaver, Dr. B.J. Bolden, Dr. Joyce A. Joyce, Dr. Bartley McSwine, Tim Seibles, J.M. Morea, Christopher Stewart, Cheryl Latif, Kelly Ellis, Duriel Harris, M. Evelina Galang, Craig Nakamoto, Oscar Brown, Jr. and the Brownhouse, Jiton Davidson, Roger Bonair-Agard, Tony Medina, and Mario. Big ups to my Oklahomies (Russ & Julie; Tod & Koren, Justin & Deb), Guild Complex, 5A Artist Management, Kendall Lloyd & Anotha Level @ Lit-X Bookstore, Tina Howell, Reggie Gibson, and Citizen King.

one.
we speak of conquest

learning to swim

for a teacher in need of permanent vacation

his sleeves rolled up tight revealing veins popping
blood pressure rising like his voice like the sound
of a broken yardstick slammed against a desk
where questioning hormones reflect
the tension of yesterday's drive-by
the glass shattered in rage from slamming the door
too hard to not notice the sweat veiling red eyes
the tears escaping quietly to the floor
where one bright-eyed fourth grader gasps for air

she knows the right answer

she is drowning

breathing room

teachers lounge
in the tiny space
between math and microwave.

we speak of Jesus
and All My Children
with equal compassion.

a small black and white
battles the static.
its foil antenna
receives mixed messages.

a half empty vending machine
squats impatiently in the corner.

but the bell chimes its piper's song
urging us reluctantly
toward the future.

private school

more lies
for people
who can afford
them.

walking shoes
notes on the 1/18/94 Klan march thru Springfield, IL.

nights of ignorance and hatred
followed by mornings
of chalk and blackboard.

i stand in a classroom
full of size fives and eights
confronting the mental warfare
on the battlefield for tomorrow's reality.

this ground, tainted
by the red on your hands
and my kin.

bleeding hearts are skin deep
but consciousness is a birthright
that grows within
since that day in 1964
when i was given these walking shoes.

many have marched
for my right to choose:
a 20 below sidewalk in springfield
or six hours in a cabrini-green house of learning.
both roads paved by drinking gourd followers
who traveled the same path.

southside rain

southside rain visits darkened corridors
falls through cracks where children dream
falls through cracks of textbook lies
and dampens hungry minds

southside rain collects in poison puddles
on playgrounds of potholed wishes
these schools are just treading water
and washing belly empty upon the pavement

we've brought the sky down on us
we've brought the sky
acid rain flows through my veins
some wonder why
(and the rain keeps falling)

southside rain seeps through unstable foundations
divides where there's no shelter
conquers where there's no hope
and mildews the rotting floor

southside rain is tears on the angel's face
searching for a place to rest
waiting for a time of truth
so her moans can cease

southside rain drops like false prophets
southside rain drops like my brother's blood
southside rain drops like our leaders
southside rain drops like my knees

our sons

for the seven and eight year old boys wrongly accused in the murder of eleven year old ryan harris

the difference between
the truth and a lie

separates a one inch skull
fracture and a rock
chucked by a seven-year old.

blue beads grip
his braids, jerking
as he nods in response.

if he grows up
he hopes to join
chicago's finest gang.

they drive fast cars,
carry big guns,
always live on tv.

just a few more questions, ma'am.

the wooden bench
no more comfortable
than it has ever been.

in chicago, justice is
a room with no windows.

her boy, seven, is hungry,
confused. she can feel it
from the muffled hallway.

door cracked. dark
as frantic shadows.
daddy is not allowed

to enter the station.
guards hold back
fire. the englewood moon

a pale, knowing bulb.

the boys, low-rent refugees
from third world corners,
bend, then break: confess

over happy
meals, they will be
forgotten like quiet bicycles.

passage

I.
sirens scream another nighttime episode
as moisture clings
to telephone wires, shimmer
a glittery dance to pulsing red and blue
illuminescence
tired steps, familiar tunes
like the busstop turned electric slide
city rhythms a sad repetition
reborn at every sunset

II.
six young bloods inhabit the corner
of division and green
we reek in concrete colors
and smell
full of bull
or so read the epitaphs
on the forty ounce tombstones
at our feet

these city nomads adjust heavy burdens
to balance against the oncoming night
a nocturnal reoccurrence:
waiting on the bus
waiting on the hands to move
waiting on change
waiting on justice
waiting on tomorrow
silently praying for warmer days

III.
we speak of conquest
as the sky sings our broken dreams
to dead homies
we check our manhood momentarily
as the westbound bus lurches into darkness
we stand as five

the lure of phat beats
and gyrating hips
send two brotha's away
pushing kicks on pavement

after a collective pocket dig
two strike enough gold
for another malt liquor ride
the bright lights leading them on

alone
one discovers pen and paper
and tries to hide
behind his words

all of us gone
in search of our fathers
in different direction

likeness

deep in father's eyes
for the first time
he found sister
the soft roundness of her way
their pupils searching

for a fleeting second
a wink
he saw brother stumbling
blood-red pleas
crying in worn footsteps

for the first time
he didn't look away
cloaking a twisted family tree
nooses dangling from scattered branches

deep in father's eyes
he didn't look away
the image was still

at home

my weary urban eyes fall.
she tries to remove the pain.
then, wishing they were clear
again, returns them.

southwestern sunlight
masquerades as warmth.
big city endless winters lie still.

words come easy.
syllables many.
yet a-b-c's seem closer
than m-f-a's
or d-a-d's.

i am a child
in your house.

the woolworth's poem
for Russ and Tod

I.
we rode summer on ten speeds
bike routes to the courthouse lawn
where parking meter hitching posts
lined melting, technicolor days.

II.
we knew every corner
from the bird droppings in the basement
to the scent of musty popcorn.

III.
we laughed in the face of history.
him, golden locked and chubby nosed.
me, bubbling hot fudge.
we dared lunch counters innocently.
so close some thought us lovers.
we were.

IV.
the parakeets and canaries are no more.
silence creeps the arthritic escalator.
those fat, pasty, sandwich fingers
labor now in snaptight kitchens
across town, their tenderness lost.

V.
Tod gave me a coffee mug
on the last day of business
before it became a museum.
he sat where freedom's students
wore ketchup and abuse
in a pre-jordan north carolina.
it is a simple mug.
opaque, speckled clay.
rounded handle.
sides geometrically balanced. sturdy.
it meant a lot to him
to give it to me.
it meant a lot to me to have it.

concrete cowboy

winchester street was loaded.
children drunk on 101 degree happiness.

a golden and wise elder sits stoically
atop his throne in this kingdom of pestilence.
hawking the block.
it's all he has.
numbering his days
in the way cartridges are dumped.
one at a time.
counting the seconds until impact.
waiting for the thud
the smell of blood.

sauntering into another friday evening.

"settle down, little man"
any daddy says.
any daddy
who is bought and sold
by an ideal
which incarcerates on notion
enslaves on downpression
and feeds on blood.

any daddy calms the four-year-old
squirming under the safety belt.
wearing western civilization tightly.
a little boy lost in a big man's boxer shorts.
sammy jr. leaps from the car and he's strapped.
brandishing two blue plastic .57 magnums.

sunlight sparkling the barrels.
justice found in every chamber.
sammy jr. takes the sidewalk
beaming at a stranger
in an even stranger land
sauntering down winchester
on a friday evening.
those two, hot, plastic pieces
come to life in tiny hands.
stretching his arms as far as they will reach
he confronts the stranger.

BLAM! SMOKED!
DUSTED! WASTED!

bombarded with shrapnel.
memory's debris.
history's disposables.
wounds cutting deeper
than a four years young
could possibly understand.
he rests the guns in his holster
and any daddy says
"now son, don't shoot at people."

hyphen

take the hyphen out
the middle
of my identity
and stick it
to the whole

half and half in half
doesn't even make three-fifths
but a fraction of bad multiplication
ruins the formula

homogenized culture
high in fats
high in saccharin
low in truth and
ready for the tasteless test:
clarence thomas

unorganic
antiseptic takes
on the hyphen
in the middle

this hyphen a clever trickster
providing certain unalienable rights
to brand names and
a false sense of security:

God, the father
God, the son
God, the dollar

america, america
the bastard stepchild
is afraid of her children

we are
afrikans, we
raise afrikans, we
rise afrikans

and knock the hyphen unconscious

name calling
a poem about female genital mutilation

the villagers carry themselves comfortably.
abundant tradition glistening
wealth from the new old ones.

> *europeans scissor the continent*
> *carving motherland sculptures*
> *with alabaster, praying hands.*

> savage, barbaric, dark continent.

souls kneeling homeward.
direction now distanced.
watered down memories drifting.

> *once tied under and open*
> *america mounts her and*
> *gives birth to a nation.*

> savage, barbaric, dark continent.

customs rust with age.
brittle trusts rupture tomorrow.
family lies in waiting.

> *she is used up and slow now*
> *with regal finger pointed*
> *they name her africa.*

> savage, barbaric, dark continent.

two.
faded at the corners

the wait

they stand in the alcove
entrance to exodus
spending time like chumps
changing bottles
old souls drift
from corner to corner

Leroy was here
when they first moved in the building
forty-five years ago
when his goatee and scruff
were but a prayer of machismo
a bloodline to brotherhood

a lifetime later
his face is full
memories
triumphs
pain
hair

they are moving out
Leroy is still here
he asked them to leave
the sign
such comfort found
in five blue words:
chicago council for community change

still life

her face like a roadmap...

traveling through years and tears
in a moment which ceases to leave.

what could he do?

what's a boy to do
with the weight of worlds
when he's still nursing?

thirty-seven years
is much too long
to be on the bottle.

once, he day-dreamed of flight.
she would sit beside him.
they would sit together.

now, punch-drunk and feet failing
he is hopelessly grounded.

she cannot be found.
she's out looking for him.

finds him.

"nogoodsorryassniggas!"

finds him in the face
of every startled stranger.

"hitmeagaindammitandseeifidontkillya!"

she finds him at every corner
traveling through years and tears
in a moment which ceases to leave.

tracks
scene at 71st and dorchester

pretty as a picture this
image faded at the corners
sepia four-chord tones
circa 1930, only it's nineteen-ninety
now howling winds moan
a dusty, pregnant sorrow
at that place where tracks
meet hard black road
way off on the otherside of last night
when he spun like an empty bottle and
sought somewhere else to lay his hat
down the line, the whistle blows knowingly
her companion rests at her feet
brittle, worn from walking
they pause between rails
stretching endlessly southward
to disappear with the sobering sun.

the dog looking for his best friend.
the sista looking for her dog.

six strings strum a sad sermon.

sixty-third & cottage grove

a new abandoned canopy promises
ghost train rides while providing refuge
from the backstabbing moonlight

twenty-four hour corner summit
meeting midnight minds inside workshirts
stained beyond weary demands for attention

greasy spoons fall by the northside
neon flickering convenience and no surprise
amidst the despair are smiles
true enough to call home

working women wait on tips gracefully
side-stepping after dinner invitations
heads held high, serving retort

salmon patties pepper p.m. hunger pangs
addressing eggs scrambled beyond indifference
as is our waitress, with too many tables

seventy-first & king drive

night smells catfish crispness
while sista girl works them curls
s's lounge buzz and slam
as brothas basehead
brothas boomin
basshead brothas boomin
base boomin
boomin bass
blowin the plastic in the used-to-be back window
a baby boppin in the backseat

jackie's restaurant is always open
well, in july, until 11:30 pm
urban queens with newport lips
hardened softness serving biscuits of like texture

leo's flowers, a fading pastel
succumbs to evening's wings
chicken wings

wild irish the bouquet of the 'hood

rogers park

at times like now
when words seem a chore
and 71st street a city away
images roll by yawning september days
to dance against lakeside dusk.

poetry is hard to find here
save that wizened oak
crying seasonal tears.

ambivalent leaves ride the air
the avenue a sea of autumn.
i rake words into piles
and dive into a welcome blanket.

postcards from bridgeport, 1997

"I would march up to Bridgeport and burn down every white person's home."

"As long as they don't cause trouble with me or my homies, I don't care what they do."

> Two sixth grade male students
> from a public school on Chicago's northside

I.
on the eve of assassination
late march grieves winter's passing.
her dense blanket sags toward earth
baiting the feral buds of spring.

II.
in school today, we wondered
if raising another devil
would dampen the flames
of an idling southside playground.

III.
like your trousers, shorty
we're loose,
but we're not free.

IV.
some say we destroying God's earth.
aunt rubie say, "naaah
God's work is always.
we destroying each other."

san antonio blue

sunday hung out by the corner
with nowhere to go.
without concern
for changing events
or turning stomachs.
brotha's huddling in a parking lot
passing a spliff
and eating church's chicken.
you weren't home.

crescent, ok.

the true sense of humankind's will
to live
is based upon grey days
and early december chill.
when stagnant pools
staid collections
and last week's tears
evolve from slouching drizzle.

skies of sunday's melancholia.
highway seventy-four south.
quilted patches of green
brown
red
weave the horizon in a cyclical blaze
of rusting ingenuity.

lonely intersections spontaneously pocket
elusive moments of congregation.

standing still
is a tempo.

three.
fortune in their eyes

roulette

in a cleveland mall
there is a bodega
known as the lottery shop.
it is grey and cramped.
the wall behind the numbers machine
is packed with shiny nicotine.
on the store shelves
are pork rinds, potato chips
cookies, and creme puffs.
cellulite-blessed women stand in line.
fortune in their eyes.

writer's block at 33 1/3

somewhere i have never been,
this address.
this lonely corner, crowded
by myself. i have this
pen. this journal collecting
footsteps. a son who is new
everyday. the love of a goddess
closeby. i have this

pen. this journal, kinder
than e-mail, though no warm embrace.
ours are bittersweet relations: when
we cannot find one another,
i am lost.

baggage

When you turn the corner
And you run into yourself
Then you know that you have turned
All the corners that are left.
                    —Langston Hughes, "Final Curve"

what if you woke up one day and
all of your blemishes had left you?

your poor judgement calls.
your lack of good sense.
a lifetime of mistakes
parading around the living room
as you stare in slack-jawed awe.

the money you stole from between your parent's mat-
tresses while looking for the true detective magazines.

the distress call you sent out on cb radio that hailed
ten unhappy truck drivers to your front door.

the lie you told your lover
to conceal your other lover.

would you let them depart?
slipping through any available orifice
leaving you lightheaded and stain free?

or would you collect them,
while struggling to remember

the stuff that makes us whole.

going down

with massive love and respect to Peter Tosh, O.M.

he give me a sideways look.
me speak anyways.
space so small, nuttin' else to do really.
elevators do have a way of humblin' people.
anxious, he stare above the door
as if tha' sinkin' lights
depend on his eyesight.
he musta pushed that button six times.
maybe it feel good to him
pokin' at tha' plastic bubble
stubbin' his finger like a toe.
nevermind tha' fact tha' elevator ignore him.
act like he ain't even there.
he still in here wid me.
me still in here wid him.
him need more patience.
him need a new job.
him need a big fat philly
joe jones roll and stop
behind a cool muted trumpet solo.
"downpressor man, where you gonna run to?"

fat-free

"The next time you hear 'smooth jazz,' ask yourself what's been smoothed over."

—Fareed Mahluli Abdul-Wahhab

pacific northwest caucasian cats
purr suburban tones
from ivory mountaintops.
the valley grows restless.

on the backsides of bechet, 'trane,
kenny g slides down mt. rainier.
asks us to help him up.
holds notes beyond his memory

on D.O.P.E.
for JC. , Derv, and the band

standing still, 'cept my head
staring at the sound inside
my brain washed in vivid colors
virulent reds seeping through
the cacophony in reach of blues
heavy textures
cranium crunching paint sticks
alive with amplified emotions
and manic movements
nappyvision never blurry
it's just my head

the GAP at haight and ashbury

the sun smiles on haight street
while hipsters wear themselves
on their sleeves
and scream for attention
in a noisy 'hood.

a pair of constables
(overdressed and out of fashion)
stand like parking meters lacking change.
a native and two nappyheads pass
in time to hear one expire:

"The Summer of Love$_{(TM)}$ is over."

these guys have never been to chicago
where july heat climbs
like the murder rate.
passion's hues harsher than tie dye.

a sign from houston

the billboard read:
guns kill dreams, hopes and people,
sponsored by joe's shooting gallery

four.
on things unborn

birth of an ancestor

for Olukunde Bwamige Nile Elazar Myles Lansana

senegal. mississippi.
ghana. alabama.
oklahoma. dahomey.
florida. yoruba.
texas. kemet.

the earth which forms your being
is seasoned with journey.

where have you been?

the distance between
womb state and dream state
close enough that you can hear
the flutter of angel's wings.

a feather tickles your face
in sleep, you smile.

what mysteries will you reveal?

the Creator murmurs your spirit,
gentle elder. you know
yesterday, today. all
about us.

we await wisdom.

all of you

for Onan Jahleel Myles Lansana

i study the path of your becoming.

dogon helix & middle
passage. trail of tears.
migration. a minneapolis
hotel room. light in closed
eyes.

you chose us, then hurried
here, all at once. again
we prayed. you withheld
breath. waited to cry

together. in that long moment
we realized our strength:
how much we overcome
to get where we're going.

beautiful one, beautiful one,
welcome.

womb

for Emily and Zahra

despite callous red clay earth
indifferent rain, fragile dirt

amidst mourning weed, thistle
wind sobs its tale, the reed whistles

through ageless summits, giving
plains, abundant, fruitful living

our ancestors created kinship with soil
for you and i to flourish, to toil

when the sun is high in its lofty vault
we sing, it's the Creator's fault

and

when the moon is milky expanse
we are dervishes, golden robed in chance

in evening years our shadows follow
the stubborn, jagged terrain of tomorrow

gently quraysh, clumsy gardener at night
these flowers blossom in the way of light

patchwork

we have abandoned our loom.
no strings attached.
tapestry weakened by worldly strain.
torn this way and that.
led by the infectious tug
which splits the difference
we make when we are whole.
not fringes in the fabric.
when rifts are deep
hands can grow idle.

i look at my hands.
i see for miles and myles.
these appendages have lived four thousand lives
have raised the earth from kenya to kentucky
have defended both projects and pyramids
have touched the lifeforce of passing spirits, and
in an effort to find a solid grasp
have ripped the tapestry.

my sistas clutch forgotten rainbows.
more of my brothas holding black steel.
do we continue to tear the fabric
or with umoja
piece the fragments together.

our loom is Mama Afrika.
our loom is her scattered watoto.
our loom is in our hands.

reflection

sometimes when i laugh
i see my mama smiling
all teeth and happy

i smiled

i saw in your face
the afternoon sky resting
on a green hillside.

way down south
inspired by EMHL and Georgia O'Keefe

i'm not afraid of your eyes anymore
in them, i see myself
brown and inviting
freeing me from shackles

your hands hold promise
hold guidance
hold me
my tongue finds your palm
your palm finds a river

it's not the power of chocolate thighs
wrapping my presence in
sweetcandiedyamsdrippingcobblermashed
potatocustardpiefrenzy
that makes me weak
makes me strong
makes me weak
makes me strong

or full lips
where breathy prayers
linger
then slither
around my insides

it's not your luscious hips
which give way to lineage
give way to survival
give way to my indecision

i have found my way to you
not a moment too soon
your subtle inquiries
bite at my ear
burning like southern heat

our scents mingle
gregariously work the room
spill out of closed doors
mix with morning
spring in the air

we travel backroads
ooing and aahhing at every change
in scenery
the sun revealing imprints
that glisten upon our skin
the peach trees now in full bloom

Georgia is always lovely this time of year

visiting

an exquisite corpse co-authored by Rachel Beck

mama earline's salmon patties make me sing
fleshy tones of pink soul, though "croquette" is french
and therefore not particularly soulful. on my own, i tire
of the same old macaroni, even with suggested
    variations.
no recipe exists for her soul-laden
plates, hot, dripping alabama.
eating here is a journey into memory
to sundays around the table after a too-long sermon.
we congregate, salivating moans
dripping prayers in kool-aid afternoons,
sitting feet up. even now, i enjoy the sweetness,
the grape-stained lips left behind.
stove-top rituals pause;
gravity tugs our eyelids.

mirror image
for Tina

afrika just got a job.
she washin' hair down at sista's beauty shop.
she step one of the lye.
she stuff her roots in a net.
she say she'll try to bring 'em home.

queen mother

for Gwendolyn Brooks

I.
a humble, quiet tiger
we delight in your knowing roar

II.
igniter of mind riots
you bask in the maelstrom
watching us loot and ransack

aunt rubie goes to market

she needed a few things
but, not much
pushing her wooden cane
against february's attitude

the tiny steps of a giant
steps which taunt forever
those beige, thick-soled shoes
bearing just over a pound per year

across seventy-ninth street
she sits at the busstop
unmoved by the wait
ninety years wise

when the bus arrives
she sits at the front
so she can see everything

she does

one hundred blocks later
the driver helps her out
her mouth still moving
the mall growing anxious

shoppers scurry around her
but, she is not concerned
aunt rubie needed a few things
but, not much.

homemade

i was made in st. stephens church
on choir pews behind an ageless pulpit.
under the almighty eye of mutha,
my cousins and i, led by aunties,
crafted stodgy hymns into poetry
with the love of God and song.

al green coloured saturday's song,
but flickering spirits painted church
sundays in deep human poetry.
our voices reached the oak pulpit,
then the small congregation, while aunties
bonnell and maudell stirred mutha

to rock and hum their gentle music. mutha
raised seven children on gospel song
and hard work. my mama, two uncles, & four aunties
talked with God in a tiny texas church
where an easy-tongued preacher stroked the pulpit,
sharing scripture as hereditary poetry.

between prayers they tilled poetry
with blood and sweat. in the garden, mutha
produced converts from her earthen pulpit:
stubborn tomatoes. melons ripe with tender song.
praising the hallowed floor of this church,
this land that knows my uncles and aunties

by name. led by my soulful aunties,
the family left calvert, texas, to inspire poetry
a little further north. they found a church

home in a place called enid, then sent for mutha.
this tired soil, this birthplace of mama's song
was now a fond rememberance, a lonely pulpit.

the space between preacher and pulpit
remains sacred. one of my aunties
now resides there, naturally. her song
full of light. her love like the poetry
of my sons' laughter. i feel mutha
everywhere. i know she's always church.

kneeling at church, i consider the pulpit,
dream about mutha and cherish my aunties.
a narrow rift divides poetry and song.

icons

we migratory birds.
we fly
high as our songs carry
our burdens to JAH.

we jitter bugs.
we dance
our stories flowing rhythm
movements forever changing.

we mood indigo.
we cool
screaming public tears
that fall for no one.

we soul food.
we greens.
collards feed us roots.
dollars bring us swoosh

we doubled over.
we down
low 'coz AMERICA is heavy
on our backs.

we migratory birds.
we fly
high as our songs carry
our burdens to JAH.

mountaintop

The Creator carves a delicate peace.
Her etchings promise presence.
tableaus picturesque imprints.
indelibly revelatory.
I and I have been to the mountaintop.
have left Her name on things unborn
like shadows behind lazy clouds
which bear abundant secrets.
be still.
listen closely.
feel knowing in the silent breeze.
breathe.

midnight messages

filling myself with easy memories
while she fights to grasp
the echoes inside her mind.

i have returned to that place
where all is in perspective.

my grain of sand existence.

water rumbles to shore
with the energy of one
thousand souls moving.

i do not resist
but flow with the delicate
nurturing of The Creator's breath
flooding my lungs with ancient whispers.

waiting for low tide
i grow restless.

fasting on solace
i am forever hungry.

praying for peace
my knees are hard and ashen.

as she rests
to ponder midnight messages
i sit listening to ancestors
in cleansing waves.

captured iridescence
on the formal union of Russ and Julie

I.
when the sun births tomorrow
her womb full of promise.
by her side, we bend our knees.

her light, now your eyes.
his song, now in tune
for her beauty lives within.

II.
now
together
you discover
a new
one.
naturally, like water, sand and gravity
feed the ocean pearls.

precious treasure.

when one is opened
and two are found.

III.
together, shining.
together, unfolding.
together, opening.

baobab
for D.J.

and there you were
caught someplace between
the cadence of nightfall and
the syrupy moonglow.

i was wandering
in need of lightwork
when the voices from your locs
led me to your forest.

my soul ached for the security
of your outstretched branches.
your spirit a rich canopy
providing shelter from the storm.

you are a baobab
whose roots define lineage
whose hands are open enough to touch forever
whose heart recalls the pulse of earth.

whose strength is The Creator's smile.

geography

there is want in fullness
those less than delicate
contours of season

we are mudslides
sagging, spreading
forward,   supple giver
invite me to ascend the sacred
space of you

the night before tomorrow
for Emily

i have come to a new understanding
since i have come to know you
understanding anew, i have
come to know you new
understanding has come since
i have known you i
have come to understanding you since
you i have known to know
you is to come understanding
have i known you to come since understanding?
a new understanding of me has come
since i have come to know you

window
a peace offering

yesterday holds no promise
other than learning for today
things may look the same
outside the window frame
but, wind has rustled the branches
leaves have abandoned our familiar
colours fade to winter pale

peering out, i often see tomorrow
bundled up warm and tight
holding her mother's hand
she checks both ways
before crossing the street
the snow crunchy beneath her feet
she imagines walking on the moon

unlike television
this glass box captures present moments
fleeting seconds reflective in scope
because we will never be here again
like memory free from hindsight
the pane is in need of repair
there's much work to be done

these words may not be worth
the paper on which they're written
they may not be worth the chasm
that denies our dread loc
but, they represent vision to me
hand extended
window open

About the Author

Quraysh Ali Lansana is the author of a poetry chapbook, *cockroach children: corner poems and street psalms* (nappyhead press, 1995) and a children's book *The Big World* (Addison-Wesley, 1999). He is the editor of *I Represent*, and *dream in yourself*, both collections of literary works from Gallery 37, published by Tia Chucha Press (1996 and 1997, respectively). *Passage*, his poetry video collaboration with Kurt Heintz, won the first ever Bob Award from WTTW-TV(PBS).

He has been widely published throughout literary journals in the United States. His poetry has been performed as theatre with Chameleon Productions and Carving Mahogany, and broadcast on National Public Radio. Quraysh is director of Kuntu Drama, Inc. and serves on the board of the Guild Complex, where he is also the Literary Programming Coordinator. Lansana is the artistic director of nappyhead press, an independent publisher of poetry since 1995.

He has been a literary teaching artist and curriculum developer for over a decade, and has led workshops in prisons, public schools and universities throughout the country. Born in Enid, Oklahoma, Quraysh currently resides in Chicago with his wife, Emily, and sons, Nile, and Onan.